SOS - Stranded in Outer Space: The Incident

By Jason Lake

SOS – Stranded in Outer Space: The Incident
by Jason Lake

Published by Children's Telepathic Workshop

PART ONE

Living aboard a space station in a different galaxy came with its own set of pros and cons, or so the children living there would soon come to find out.

Their space station was a far-off scientific Earth outpost located in the Andromeda galaxy, stationed there with the sole purpose of research. The year was 2067, and those aboard the space station lived a peaceful existence with no real worries or threats... until the incident.

The space station itself was an adequate size for all eleven of them. It was neither too big, nor too small; pretty much just right. The only real complaint that the children had about it, however, was that it was rather drab looking. It was a space station, after all, so there weren't too many frills. It was cold and metallic with no personality so to speak, consisting mostly of gray colored metal running throughout it. Sure, there were colorful lights here and there and there were also splashes of color throughout the station, like in their bedrooms or in the kitchen, but for the most part it was just... gray. They couldn't exactly do a lot to spruce it up and so the children found it somewhat depressing and boring to be stuck there all hours of the day in a place to bleak.

Aboard the space station there were several adults and a handful of children. There was Kim, who was the mother of thirteen-year-old Jessica, both originally from the United States. Bill and Andrea, with their nine-year-old daughter Amber, hailing from the United Kingdom. Kevin and Terra along with their fourteen-year-old son Matt, all three of them also coming from the United States.

As for the childless adults, there was the mission leader, Nancy, a woman from Australia. The lead scientist, Arjun, originally from India. And finally, the cook, Paolo, coming from Brazil.

The children were close enough in age that the difference between them didn't matter all that much; sure, Jessica and Matt were both teenagers and Amber was barely hitting double digits. But at the same time, they were all each other really had in terms of peers, and so they all got along without too many problems. They still argued and fought and disagreed of course, but nothing out of the ordinary for kids their age.

The day that everything changed, unsurprisingly started off as normal as any other day. The kids got up, had something to eat, got ready, had virtual school, and then had leisure time after everything was said and done. There wasn't a whole lot to do aboard the space station due to the lack of space and resources and so they often had to get creative when finding something to do, whether it be make up a new game, talk online and communicate with those down on Earth, learn more and help their parents out with whatever they could, or simply just play video games and spend time together. Or, their last and final option, gripe and complain about how little there was to do... which was what ended up happening on that day.

"I hate being up here sometimes," Amber began, sighing as the three of them sat in their shared living space. She sat on a small couch by herself, her legs crossed and her head in her hands as her eyes glanced across the room and out the small window that they had, showing outer space and the distant stars. "Everyone said it'd be so fun and exciting, but there's nothing to actually do up here other than to just sit around all the time."

"And there are people on Earth complaining about the same exact thing right now, that there's nothing to do despite having the whole Earth to explore," Matt pointed out. "Always have been and probably always will be."

"Yeah, but at least they actually have the whole Earth to roam. They could just hop in a car or on a plane or a train or whatever and go somewhere new and exciting, just because. They could go anywhere and experience anything! But what do we have to do?" Amber sighed, defeated. "Walk the same gray hallways? Eat the same food because we can't grow a lot of new things? Play the same video games that we always do?"

"Sure, they have the entire Earth to roam," Matt began. "But most of them just stay in one place waiting for something to come to them and become irritated when nothing does. And so, they too fall into the same cycle that you have, limiting yourself by thinking that there's nothing to actually do."

Jessica snorted hearing this. "And when did you get to be so wise?" She joked, knocking him in the shoulder as the two of them sat on the same couch together across from Amber. Her feet were propped up on the coffee table in front of them as she laid back, relaxing into the couch. "You turn fourteen and suddenly know the answer to all of life's questions. Will the same thing happen to me?"

"I'm not being wise; I'm just pointing out that it feels like she's limited because we're stuck up here and the space here is tiny compared to Earth. But in reality, what would you even be doing if we were down on Earth right now?" Matt asked Amber. "You don't think that you'd just be sitting around just like this, bored out of your mind wishing that you were somewhere else doing something else?"

"If I were down on Earth..." Amber trailed off, pondering, as the question had caught her off guard. "I don't know! Maybe I'd go to a shopping mall. Or an ice cream place. Or get pizza with my friends. Or even just walk around outside and get to experience fresh air and the sun. Even just sitting outside with the sun and a breeze is something nice to do, and instead we're stuck here on this spacecraft with these stupid gray walls and lifeless environment!" Amber scorned. "If I look outside, all I see is the same black sky passing me by over and over again."

"And on Earth, the sky is blue with clouds. It doesn't really change all that much," Jessica joked. "Come on, let's go find something to do so you don't sit here grumpy for the rest of the day."

"No, there's nothing to do," Amber crossed her arms and pouted.

"Amber," Jessica frowned as she stood up and held out a hand, motioning for Amber to take it. Amber looked up, still grumpy, and hesitantly took it before walking off with Jessica. She wasn't happy about it but knew that there was no point in objecting and throwing an even bigger fit. After all, all three of them felt the same to some degree.

They could only help their parents out so much, could only learn so much without getting burnt out or bored. And it wasn't like they could really make new friends all that well, either; the communications with Earth took a while due to them being so far away in space, and so any friends that they had online were more like pen pals that they wrote to occasionally. Except instead of a traditional pen pal, the kids didn't have much new ever going on in their lives and therefore didn't have too much to talk about. When people found out they were in space on a research mission, they often thought it was so exciting... until the kids would write back the truth of the matter and the pen pal would slowly lose interest.

With Jessica trying to find something to do with Amber, this left Matt alone by himself in their common living area, although he didn't particularly mind. He was at an age where he would sometimes rather be left alone with his thoughts and emotions, his hormones raging through him as he transitioned from a child to a teenager. Still though, he was curious as to what they would end up finding to do, and his curiosity got the best of him. He stood up, about to follow them wherever they had gone, when something froze him in his tracks.

The familiar living room that he had spent countless hours in was suddenly bathed in an extremely bright red flashing light, alongside a loud and abrupt alarm going off at once following the lights. Matt's heart raced as he glanced around, unsure of what was going on. He glanced out the tiny window quickly only to see a large spaceship approaching, except this one looked nothing like their own.

Instead, this spaceship looked foreign, unfamiliar. It was certainly not designed by anyone on Earth, or so he assumed. But who could be approaching them in such a manor? They had clearance for this research space station after all... from Earth at least. They had been living there for a good amount of time without any issues... had something changed? Was the approaching ship in danger and needing help?

That's what Matt wanted to think was happening, but a certain unease filled his being as he took in the few details he could see from the cramped window. Something about the new spaceship felt malicious, unwanted... but he couldn't exactly figure out why.

"Matt!" Jessica yelled, running into the room, Amber no longer with her. "Come on, what are you doing just standing there?"

"I don't... I don't know what's going on," Matt replied loudly to speak over the alarm, taking in how frazzled Jessica looked. Her hair was loose and wild, a peculiar look of fear and worry gleaming in her eyes. She seemed almost out of breath, even though Matt didn't think that she had made it far with Amber. Besides that, she seemed to be fine physically, which put him at ease even if it was just a little bit.

"Why aren't you listening to the alarm?" Jessica asked, annoyed as she took quick strides and walked over, grabbing him by the hand and nearly yanking his arm out of its socket. "I can barely even hear anything over it!"

Matt took a second to actually listen to the alarm, only to realize that it had been transmitting a message the entire time and for some odd reason, whether it be shock or some other reason, his brain hadn't been processing it. It essentially was informing the adults to take security measures and it was playing on repeat. Once he finally heard it, he was in shock that he hadn't noticed it in the first place. It pierced his eardrums and was unbelievably loud as it rang out.

Matt followed Jessica as the two of them ran down the hallway, no longer holding her hand but still keeping up with her. "Where is everyone?" he asked.

"The adults took Amber to hide in some secret spot," Jessica replied. "It's near the kitchen; I never knew about it, but I guess that they did. It's to hide in for emergencies," she explained, shouting to be heard over the alarm.

Matt hadn't heard of it either but thought that it made sense. If there was an emergency aboard the ship, he figured that one of their top priorities would most likely end up being their survival, meaning food and shelter, so having an emergency hiding spot in or near the kitchen made the most sense. At least that way, they could wait things out even if the rest of the craft was destroyed until someone hopefully saved them.

Still, he didn't understand what was truly going on and his heart continued to pound harder and harder in his chest, part from fear and the other part being from running across the ship to seek shelter. What was even going on in the first place? Would everyone be okay? Was this all just a drill, or was something actually going on? He wondered but didn't want to say it out loud and make Jessica even more tense and stressed out. After all, they had lived a relatively peaceful existence aboard the space station for so long that he could never even imagine something going wrong like this, so Matt was hoping that this was all just a drill of some kind.

They eventually made their way to the entrance of the shelter; Terra, Matt's mother, was waiting outside of it with an anxious look on her face and her arms crossed. Once she made eye contact with Matt, it melted away ever so slightly, and she rushed to embrace him.

"Matt," she breathed, hugging him tightly. "Thank god you were able to make it here,"

"Why? What's going on?" Matt asked, hugging her back, confused.

"We don't have a lot of time to explain, okay sweetie?" She brushed his hair to the side with her hand, looking into his eyes deeply and lovingly. "Just know that I love you, and your father loves you too, okay? No matter what happens, please hold that close to you."

"Mom, this sounds way too... final," Matt bit out. "This is way too serious. Can you please just tell me what's going on?"

"I wish I could, but I'm already risking everything just saying goodbye to you like this. Just... please get into the shelter with Jessica, okay?" Terra tried keeping on a brave face, but Matt knew she was distraught and on the verge of crying. "Stay safe,"

"I will, mom," Matt agreed, and Terra pulled him in for one final hug.

"Try to keep those girls safe too, okay? Promise me," she insisted as they broke apart.

"I will," Matt agreed once more, just to ease her conscious, although in the back of his mind he wondered... safe from what? Safe from who? What danger could there be, and why didn't she want to go into detail about it?

"Okay, now get in," Terra instructed him and he made his way into the hiding area, Jessica leading the way. It wasn't too cramped but would have been much more worse had all eight adults and three kids tried to pile in... which made Matt wonder, where were all the adults? What were they all doing, and if this was an emergency, why not come hide in this shelter with them?

The door shut but there was still a dim light on inside. Amber looked scared out of her mind, Jessica not doing too hot either, but Matt didn't know how to feel. The way that his mother had just spoken to him... it made him feel like he wasn't going to see her again for a long time. Like she knew this, and yet didn't tell him in the moment.

"Did she tell you anything about what's going on?" Matt whispered to Jessica, not wanting to talk at full volume out of fear.

Jessica shook her head. "No, you?"

"Not really. She just said to stay safe... she didn't even say how long we're supposed to be in here or how to really get out." Matt sighed. "I guess we just wait?"

"Nothing more we can really do," Jessica agreed, slumped on the cold floor, her back against the wall. Her eyes fluttered closed, although she knew she wouldn't actually be able to sleep any. Instead, she simply held Amber's hand tightly, trying to be a comfort for her and maybe calm her down a bit.

--

A sudden thud startled all three children.

Matt listened closely as Jessica looked over at him, wide-eyed and terrified. He couldn't get up and try to go listen without possibly compromising the fact that they were in the shelter, and so he instead tried listening as much as he could manage from where he sat. There was another thud, followed by some shuffling and odd noises that Matt couldn't recognize, before it all went quiet.

"What was that?" Jessica hissed, although clearly none of them knew what was going on.

"Well, if it was any of the adults, then they would have probably opened the door and told us we could come out," Matt replied.

"Are you trying to say it wasn't... one of the adults?" Amber asked in a hushed, terrified tone as she looked up at Matt with her soft, big eyes.

"I don't..." Matt trailed off. "I don't know. I saw a ship approaching before I ran here but it looked so weird that I didn't know what to make of it."

"Another ship? Why didn't you mention this before!" Jessica barked at him while still keeping her voice down. "I didn't see another ship!"

"Sorry, I'm just all over the place right now," Matt responded. "But yeah, it didn't look familiar... I didn't get a super good look at it though. I only saw it after the alarms started to go off."

Jessica's stomach twisted up as she realized what this could only mean. "So, is someone hijacking the space station then? Is that what's going on?" She asked, holding Amber's hand even tighter.

"I mean, if it's not someone hijacking the space station... then what could it be?" Matt said. "I just don't get why they'd put us in this room and not tell us anything. I mean, wouldn't it have been better to even just tell us something rather than nothing? Now, we're stuck in this room until who knows when."

"No one's coming to get us?" Amber asked meekly.

"We don't know that" Jessica replied. "But... if it is a hijacking and someone is aboard the space station right now to take it over or do whatever it is they're doing, then they probably just didn't tell us because we would have started freaking out and wouldn't have agreed to stay locked up in here hiding from them."

"Well, what do we do from here then?" Matt asked Jessica. There were no more sounds coming from outside, and there hadn't been in a while, but he wasn't about to open the door in the off chance of something going wrong.

"Well, we just heard someone outside maybe five minutes ago or so. So clearly, whoever it was is still on board the station, whether they're supposed to be here or not... like you said, if it was one of the adults then they probably would have let us out by now. I mean, it's been a couple hours at least since we got in here, right?" Jessica asked.

"I think so. I've been dozing off, or spacing out, I can't tell which," Matt agreed. "I think my perception of time is off right now because of it."

"Okay, so if it's someone that isn't supposed to be here, then we'll have to wait them out as long as we can. There's no bathroom in here and no food, but I think we're all okay for now," Jessica said.

"I'm fine for the time being," Matt agreed. "It's lucky that we had lunch before everything happened. At least hunger won't be that big of an issue, at least not for a little while longer."

Amber solemnly nodded. "I feel too nervous to eat anything," she admitted. "Even if I was hungry."

"Okay, so that's taken care of. So, for now, I'd say we should wait until at least the morning to start and venture out... that is, if we don't hear anything from now until then. Whoever is on the ship can't be staying here for all that long, or at least I hope they aren't. If anything, one of us can sneak out and try and figure out what's going on," Jessica suggested.

"That's pretty risky," Matt frowned.

"Well, we're going to need to go use the bathroom and get food and water at some point... and we can't live inside this closet or whatever you want to call it forever," Jessica told him.

"I guess you have a point. I just... I really don't know what the right thing to do is. I mean, my mom told me to keep everyone safe, but I don't even know how to do that honestly." Matt sighed. "I don't even understand what these people, if they are hijacking the station, what they would want."

"Maybe our parents' research?" Amber suggested. "Maybe it's important to them for some reason."

Jessica nodded. "It's the only logical reason that I could think of for them to attack us and take over the space station like this. But what could they even be researching that's so important? What would they want that information for?"

"Probably just for their own gain," Matt suggested. "They might be stealing their research to sell and pawn off to other companies or something like that."

"Why not just steal the information digitally, though?" Amber asked, confused.

"Instead of coming onto the space station they could have just stolen it like that online, right?"

"I was under the impression that all of their information was encrypted," Jessica admitted. "I don't know if any of it was even online in the first place, but it wasn't something that I ever really asked about."

"Regardless of why they're here, they are. The best we can do is just play it by ear, I think," Matt said. "I just hope nothing too bad is going on out there."

PART TWO

The three waited until the following morning to venture out of the shelter. They hadn't heard much since the thuds the previous day and assumed that meant that either whoever had boarded the ship had left or at least wasn't occupying that part of the space station.

Matt volunteered to be the first to head out, insisting that Jessica and Amber stay behind just in case he got captured. That's what they had assumed happened to their parents, anyway. They made a secret knock so that the girls would know it was safe to come out and with that being squared away, he quietly opened the door to the shelter, walking out and finding... nothing too out of the ordinary. It was the same, gray space station, as always.

"It's just this one hallway that's the same though," Matt reminded himself mentally. "Don't get too eager just because it looks like no one tampered with anything here."

Matt slowly crept down the hallway, trying his best to not make any noise. Every step he took was gentle and without noise, the only real sounds being his breathing. He felt like he was breathing heavier than normal, but figured it was just his nerves and brushed off the fear. Still though, it felt like he was struggling for each breath.

His first stop was the kitchen. He peered around the corner and saw no one. He was cautious, listening closely to hear if anyone else was there. He couldn't hear anything and proceeded to walk into the kitchen, noting that a few items of food were still out from yesterday's lunch, meaning Paolo never got the chance to clean any of it up. It felt wrong to see everything out like that, abandoned and messy, but Matt couldn't exactly put it into words why. It was as if he was looking at what used to be his former life, although he still didn't know what was actually going on.

He decided that it wasn't worth it to clean all of this up and his time would be much better spent exploring the rest of the space station. He went down the hallway, towards the main area of the station where the communications room was. At least he could communicate to Earth about the situation. Maybe they would be able to help once they found out what had happened.

With each hallway that he went down, he was extremely cautious, maybe even too cautious, waiting long amounts of time before actually venturing down just in the off chance there was someone... or something there. He slowly checked each room, and he did feel bad that he was making Jessica and Amber wait so long... but he figured that he was better safe than sorry.

By the time he had reached the communications room, he hadn't found too much out of place or anything to really indicate what had happened. With a shaky hand, he opened the door to the communications room, uncertain of what he'd find beyond only to see the entire room... destroyed.

"No," he breathed out in disbelief. "This can't be."

All the screens, holograms, keyboards, were smashed to pieces. There was no communicating with Earth and telling them what had happened. And the harsh reality of the situation hit Matt, hard.

He ran his hands through his hair, trying not to cry. They were stranded in space in a different galaxy with no way to communicate, and on top of that, it was simply him and two other girls that were younger than him. They were just a bunch of kids thrust into such a heavy situation that he didn't know how to react, his chest felt like it was about to collapse, and he started to hyperventilate.

He paced back and forth, trying to start up any of the communications geat. The only panel that was still somewhat operational was the one showing the status of the ship, but everything seemed to be fine there. He wasn't too familiar with using the communications system, but if that was the only thing really operational, then maybe he could try and communicate out through it somehow.

He started messing with the panel, only for an error message to suddenly flash on the screen. "Warning", it read. "Low oxygen. System due to fail in approximately twenty-three minutes based on current oxygen use."

Matt's heart sank and in that moment, he knew why his chest had hurt so much, why every breath felt like he was breathing through a straw. Because the oxygen was about to be entirely depleted.

"But how?" He wondered to himself as he took off sprinting to Jessica and Amber. "Did whoever come aboard the space station do this? Or is it a genuine malfunction?"

His chest felt like it was about to cave in by the time he had reached the shelter, and he panted heavily outside the door as his left arm feebly knocked their secret code. Jessica opened the door at once as Matt clung to the wall outside, lightheaded.

"What's wrong?" Jessica exclaimed. "Why are you breathing like that?"

"The oxygen," Matt began but immediately coughed, hard. "The oxygen is about to run out," he repeated once he was able to get a deep breath in.

"Run out?" Amber asked, worry setting in in her face even more so than before.

"Well let's go to the oxygen system and try and restart it then," Jessica insisted before taking them both by the hand. Amber, because she was scared, and Matt, because he could barely stand on his own two feet at that point without the risk of blacking out.

Jessica quickly made her way to the room that hosted the oxygen systems as she hastily yanked both of them along, fear and panic setting in and making a bed in her heart. It was the one time she was grateful that the space station was so small; getting to the oxygen room took no time at all, and they were going to need every second.

By the time that they got to the room, a red light similar to the one from yesterday had started up and was flashing, although the alarm wasn't as severe and overpowering as yesterday. "Low oxygen," it rang out.

"I'm already working on it," Jessica spat back despite it just being an automated message, making Amber giggle for the first time in what felt like forever.

Jessica herself didn't have a whole lot of experience with the systems, but her mother, Kim, had shown her the basics just in case of an emergency. One of the things that she had shown her specifically had been how to restart the oxygen in case the system had malfunctioned for whatever reason; she said it was best to start with that, and if there were any issues from there then they'd take care of it.

Jessica quickly worked to restart the system, her hands shaking and beads of sweat running down her face. The flashing red lights weren't helping much and were making her anxiety even worse. She hadn't realized how hard it was to breathe until she had stopped moving, her lungs unable to actually breathe in enough oxygen all at once, or so it felt. Her hands quickly worked to reset everything, but her anxiety was ultimately getting the best of her. If she was able to fix the system, then everything would be okay, or at least it would for the moment.

If not, they died.

Matt was slowly getting his own wind back but knew he would only get in the way if he tried to jump in, and so he observed her at work. He was grateful whoever had overtaken the ship hadn't destroyed the oxygen room; at least this way, if they fixed it, they could survive another day and try to figure out what to do.

"Alright, I think that's everything," Jessica called out over the alarm. "I just have to press this last button and it should work... hopefully," she added, before hitting the final button with her fingers crossed.

The air in the room was still and tense as they all looked around with expectant eyes. It was a few moments before the system came on, announcing, "Oxygen scrubbers restarted. Oxygen production back to 100%."

The three kids sighed out a breath of relief, Jessica nearly melting to the floor as her lower back felt as though it was about to give out. "Thank god," she nearly cried, wiping her eyes. "I can't believe I actually did it."

They all huddled together, holding each other as the severity of the situation hit them. Sure, they had fixed the oxygen and that was more than enough reason for celebration. But they weren't out of the woods yet... far from it.

Afterwards, they made their way back to the communication room so that Matt could show them what had happened. "I'm assuming they broke this before they left," he told Jessica and Amber. "I don't know if they knew we were on board, but regardless we can't contact anyone... or at least, I don't think that we can."

"Are you able to see the surveillance footage?" Amber asked. "Maybe we can find out who actually came on board if they didn't destroy that too."

"I didn't even think of it," Jessica admitted before getting to work.

They were able to pull up the past twenty-four, hours of surveillance footage, and their chests felt tight as they fast-forwarded through everything that had happened. The three of them in the living area, before everything had gone downhill. Their parents, unsuspecting of everything to come. Paolo in the kitchen, just starting to clean up from lunch.

They watched as a door suddenly opened and a group of... aliens emerged! Jessica's mouth hung wide open as she stared on in disbelief, Matt's eyes wide and Amber clutching her mouth. There had been aliens aboard the ship, and the three of them didn't even know it.

They felt sick to their stomachs but kept watching as the aliens took their parents hostage and forced them off the ship. They then watched as they destroyed the communications room, talking amongst themselves in a language that none of the kids recognized or could understand. Finally, they did one final sweep of the place;

that's when they had heard the thud yesterday. It had come from an alien walking outside of the shelter, and they sat there in disbelief over the fact that he had gotten so close and yet they hadn’t had any idea.

"What do we do now?" Jessica asked meekly.

"We have to save our parents," Amber insisted, clearly upset. "They would do the same for us,"

"Well yeah, we should save them... but how? We don't know anything about these guys or why they even took them in the first place. If they wanted just scientists, then why take someone like Paolo?" Matt shook his head.

"There's something bigger at work here. I just wish we could talk to Earth and tell them what happened..."

He was abruptly cut off by the computer monitor lighting up and a new flashing light. "Alert," it read. "Ship en route to dock with station."

"Who is it now?" Jessica exclaimed, rushing over to try and see if they could view the docking port. On the screen, an image of a different ship that they had never seen came into view as it slowly docked.

"I don't recognize the ship," Matt told her.

"What do we do then?" Amber asked, hiding behind Jessica, and clinging to her. "Do we go hide in the shelter?"

"Yeah, what do we do? Do we stand our ground?" Jessica suggested.

"I don't..." Matt trailed off.

"What should we do?" Jessica asked once more, the panic in her voice setting in as the ship was almost done docking. Her eyes were terrified as they glanced between the screen and Matt, her hands sweaty despite her wiping them off on her pants. Amber was trembling behind her, unsure of what to do with herself, and Matt simply looked over at the two of them with a blank, guilty look on his face.

"I don't know."

THE END

About the Author

Jason Lake was born *in the late 1970's in Omaha, Nebraska* and grew up in *Southern Colorado* learning to *live sustainably off the land.* In the early 2000's he left *Colorado* for a few years travelling the world including places like Japan, Australia, and South America all the while writing for blogs and DJ'ing in small clubs to make enough money to keep his travels going. *Jason* now lives back in *Southern Colorado* with his wife and daughters and lots of animals. When not writing, *Jason* likes to *garden, hike, and produce electronic music.*

CHILDREN'S TELEPATHIC
WORKSHOP

www.ingramcontent.com/pod-product-compliance
Lightning Source LLC
LaVergne TN
LVHW010122170826
845678LV00012B/2544

* 9 7 9 8 4 7 8 6 4 2 8 2 2 *